ROMAN FORTS

*First published in
the United States in 1990 by*
Franklin Watts
387 Park Avenue South
New York NY 10016

Back cover: Hadrian's Wall, northern England.
Design David West   *Picture researcher* Cecilia Weston-Baker
         Children's Book Design *Illustrator* Gerald Wood
Editor Catherine Bradley   *Map* Aziz Khan

The consultant, Simon James, is a specialist on Roman history and works for the Education Office at the British Museum.

Library of Congress Cataloging-in-Publication Data

Mulvihill, Margaret.
      Roman Forts / Margaret Mulvihill.
         p. cm. -- [History highlights]
      Summary: Examines the structure and defenses of an ancient Roman
fort. Roman military life, and the campaigns waged by the Roman Empire
against its enemies.
      ISBN 0-531-17201-5
      1. Fortification. Roman--Juvenile literature. [1. Roman--Army.] I. Title.
II. Series: History highlights (New York, N.Y.)
UG428.M85 1990
355.7 0937--dc20
89-28778   CIP   AC

Contents

HISTORY HIGHLIGHTS

ROMAN FORTS

GLOUCESTER PRESS
New York · London · Toronto · Sydney

INTRODUCTION

The time of the Roman Empire was one of great prosperity and peace for much of Europe, North Africa and Asia Minor. Within this vast empire's boundaries there was a common law and common official languages, Latin and Greek. In its cities and towns people of many different cultures lived as Roman citizens, their safety guaranteed by the *Pax Romana*, or Roman peace. This peace was maintained by a highly organized army. When an area came under Roman control, forts of wood and stone were built.

These buildings were bases from which soldiers could patrol far frontiers and roads, and within which they could have permanent winter quarters.

The first emperor was Octavian, whose supporters gave him the title Augustus, which means "majestic" in Latin. He was a great nephew of Julius Caesar and became emperor after a series of civil wars. Augustus reigned for nearly 50 years (until AD 14). His rule brought peace after years of strife. Augustus re-organized Roman coins, law and taxation. At the end of his reign Augustus transformed the armies that had fought the civil wars into a professional peace-keeping force, which protected the empire's frontiers.

The Roman army conducts a triumphal march through the center of Rome. Augustus boasted, with some justification, that he had found Rome a city of brick and left it a city of marble. The Forum (seen below) was the center of government.

THE ROMAN EMPIRE

At its greatest extent, during the second century AD, the Roman Empire included the whole of the Mediterranean World and stretched as far as Britain in the north and Arabia in the southwest. This huge territory included a great variety of peoples and cultures. There were the Celts, Iberians, Greeks, Egyptians and many others.

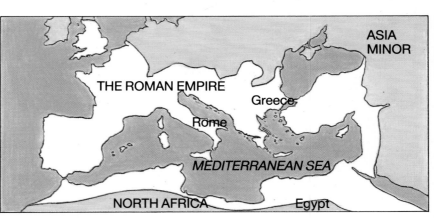

ASIA MINOR

THE ROMAN EMPIRE

Greece

Rome

MEDITERRANEAN SEA

NORTH AFRICA

Egypt

THE ROMAN ARMY

The Roman army was a well-trained and equipped body. It was organized in such a way that every soldier knew exactly what his position was and where he should fight in a battle. Augustus' army was made up of 28 legions.

The most important officers in a legion were the centurions. These captains of the Roman army carried a twisted vine stick as their badge of office – it was used for hitting legionaries – and there were about 60 centurions to a legion. Many came from the ranks and some were very brutal. There were also many technical officers, such as engineers, surveyors and medical men, as well as another army of clerks to organize how to pay, feed and equip the soldiers.

The Roman army relied on many auxiliary, or native soldiers. Numidians from Africa and Gauls from modern France were better horsemen than native Romans or Italians, and the finest archers and slingers were recruited from Crete and the Balearic Islands.

Under strict drill masters Roman recruits learned to march and run, to leap, swim and ride, and to use their weapons in attack and defense.

Every legion had a silver eagle – the symbol of the Roman Empire – as its standard. Individual units would have additional flags and badges, featuring zodiac signs or other fierce animals like wolves and boars. The loss of a standard was regarded as a disgrace and in camps and forts the legion's standards were kept in a shrine called the *sacellum*.

A ROMAN LEGION

Each Roman legion was divided into units. Ten sections of eight men made up a century. Six centuries comprised a cohort (480 men) and ten cohorts made up a legion. Each cohort had its own battle order. For example, the sixth cohort generally consisted of the youngest, fittest men, while the seventh and the ninth were the weakest cohorts. Some 120 cavalrymen were attached to each legion, and they acted as scouts and dispatch riders.

COHORTS

10 9 8 7 6 5 4 3 2 1

cavalry

5 Tribuni

Legatus

Praefectus

Aquilifer

Centurion

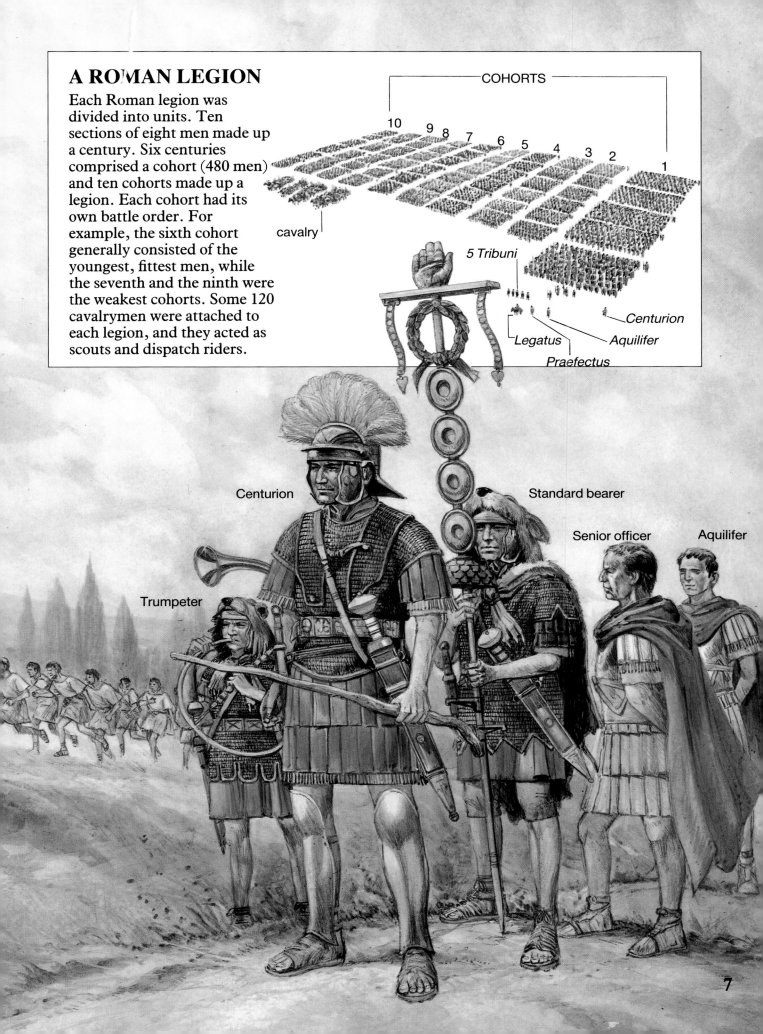

Centurion

Standard bearer

Senior officer

Aquilifer

Trumpeter

THE ROMAN SOLDIER

In the earliest days of Rome each citizen had to be prepared to fight without being paid. But soldiers in the Roman empire were paid professionals who signed on for 20-25 years of service. They had to work very hard – often marching 20 miles a day.

Living conditions were simple and very basic. In the field eight men would share a tent and a packmule; in a fort they shared just two rooms: one for sleeping in and one for storing their equipment. Much of a soldier's time was spent on patrols or on sentry duty. Soldiers would be moved around the empire as they were needed from Britain to Africa. During their army service they contributed money to a savings scheme so when they retired they could expect a gift of land or a pension. Usually the land was near the last place where they had been garrisoned. Soldiers were not supposed to marry while in service but this rule was often ignored. In time their sons might join the army as well.

Legionaries return to the fort from a patrol. During their time off duty, soldiers would play games or go to the baths. The soldiers, right, are playing with bones. Playing dice for money was not allowed but many ignored this rule. Some soldiers carried flutes and drums with their kit and whiled away the time playing music.

ARMOR AND WEAPONS

Over his woolen tunic an ordinary legionary wore a breastplate of metal strips, scales or rings. He had heavy studded sandals and a helmet. In cold conditions, during British winters, for example, he could stuff the thongs of his sandals with wool and fur and he would be issued with a heavy, hooded cloak. A foot soldier had his short sword, two javelins and a heavy, rectangular shield of leather and wood. Although there were repair workshops attached to each legion, much of the army's equipment came from Gaul and northern Italy. Weapons were made by the army and by private metalsmiths.

CAMPS AND FORTS

At the end of a day's march, Roman army units would build a stockaded camp. Surveying and engineering officers were sent ahead to find clear, level ground, which could not be overlooked by enemies, near a good supply of water.

Camps were usually square or rectangular in shape. A deep trench was dug around the site and the soil and turf were made into an embankment about 25 feet high. On top of this earth rampart the soldiers set up their stakes. Within this stockade the tents were pitched according to a regular pattern. In camps the headquarters complex included the commander and senior officers' tents, as well as the standards. The soldiers' tents were pitched in orderly rows around this area, with latrines and trash pits spaced around them.

The legionary bases followed the same fairly standard layout as the camps. The bases were permanent and often used as winter headquarters when the army was not on the move.

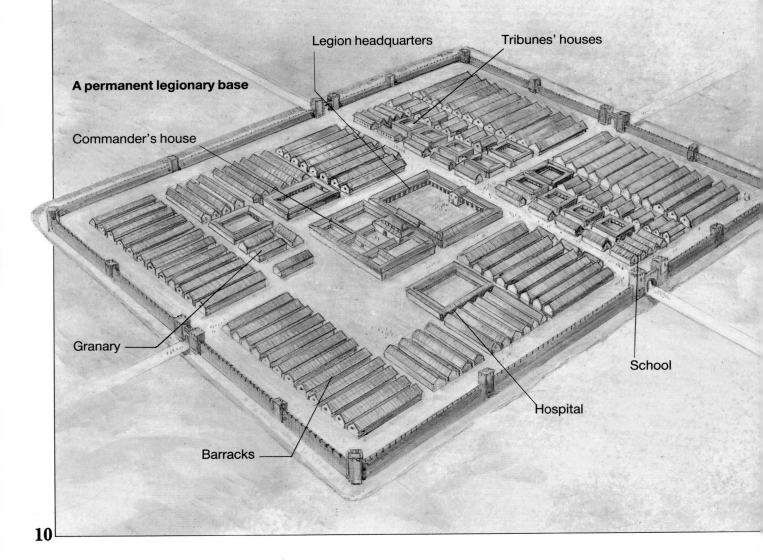

A permanent legionary base

Legion headquarters

Tribunes' houses

Commander's house

Granary

Barracks

Hospital

School

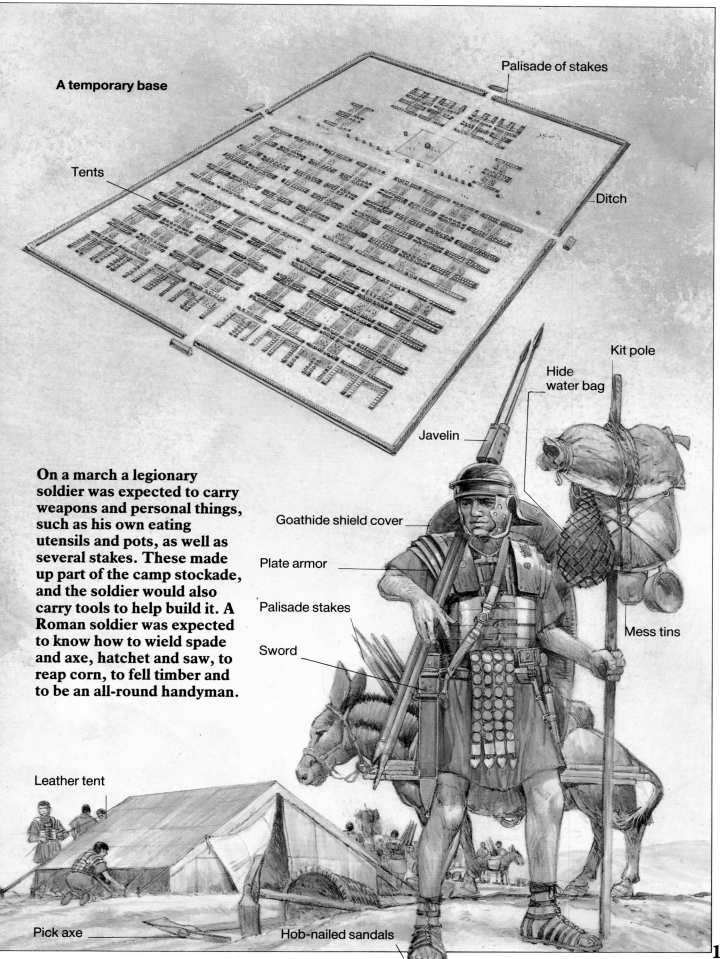

A temporary base

Palisade of stakes

Tents

Ditch

Kit pole

Hide
water bag

Javelin

Goathide shield cover

Plate armor

Palisade stakes

Sword

Mess tins

On a march a legionary
soldier was expected to carry
weapons and personal things,
such as his own eating
utensils and pots, as well as
several stakes. These made
up part of the camp stockade,
and the soldier would also
carry tools to help build it. A
Roman soldier was expected
to know how to wield spade
and axe, hatchet and saw, to
reap corn, to fell timber and
to be an all-round handyman.

Leather tent

Pick axe

Hob-nailed sandals

INSIDE A ROMAN FORT

Gradually, as the Roman Empire stopped expanding, permanent forts were built for the legions garrisoned in frontier zones. Instead of a simple stockade, these forts had stone or at least wooden walls. The ramparts were made of timber and earth. A guarded gate and watch-towers were set into each of the four walls.

As with the camps, the fort's main road led to the central headquarter (*principia*) buildings – the commander's house (*praetorium*), granaries for storing the soldiers' rations and the hospital (*valetudinarium*). In the *principia* there was often a large hall, which contained the shrine for the standards. Forts also bustled with armament workshops, stables and there was a small prison.

The basic plan had to be adjusted to take account of local conditions. In a hot African fort more room was allowed for each soldier's bed and a large courtyard served as the hall, while the British barrack block had to have a fireplace.

The Romans knew the importance of diet, exercise and hygiene for general health. Although senior officers had servants to keep house for them, the ordinary soldiers were expected to keep themselves and their quarters clean and tidy. The centurions gave out different chores, and made sure that the work was done. The soldiers below have the unpleasant duty of cleaning out the latrines.

THE BATHHOUSE

Roman soldiers were clean as well as fit. Within the bathhouses attached to every fort a soldier progressed from a tepid room to a hot room, and from the sweat room to the cold bath. The soldiers would rub oil onto their skin to clean themselves. In the hot room they would sweat and scrape the dirt off. The baths were like a clubhouse, where soldiers could enjoy a few games and a bit of gossip. Baths were usually outside the forts. This was because they needed hot water and the furnace that was used to supply the water could be a fire hazard for the fort.

DEFENDING A ROMAN FORT

Security within a Roman fort was very strict. Every day there was a different watchword which was written on waxed pieces of wood. An officer called the *tesserius* was in charge of organizing the sentries and passing on this watchword. Then, each night, four legionary cavalrymen went round to inspect the watchmen. If all was in order they took the watchwords (*tesserae*) from the sentries on duty. Then, at daybreak, the inspection party reported to the officer in charge, and handed over the wooden tablets.

If anything had gone wrong, if a sentry had been found asleep, for example, he was court-martialled. If he was found guilty he was usually sentenced to being set upon with stones and cudgels by men from his own unit. Such men usually died. If they didn't they were disgraced forever. The same penalty existed for theft. It was also considered a serious offense to lose weapons on a battlefield or to give up a position out of fear.

To communicate with other forts or units along the frontier, the Romans had elaborate signaling techniques. From special towers they issued columns of smoke from straw by day, and torch signals by night. The signaling tower had to be high enough for fire or smoke to rise clear of trees and mist. Fog made signaling impossible.

WAR MACHINES

Roman soldiers used various large war machines. A *catapulta* shot arrows. A giant catapult, the *ballista*, could hurl huge stones for 300 meters, crushing the massed ranks of the enemy or devastating the walls of an enemy fort. The most powerful catapult was the *onager*, the "wild ass," so-named because of its deadly kick. The Roman army also used low sheds and high towers on wheels. Within these machines gangs of soldiers could dig at the foot of an enemy fort's wall, weakening the foundations, or get near enough to scale them.

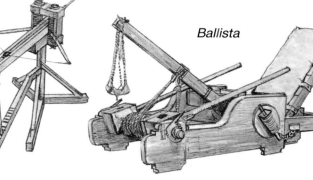

Catapulta

Ballista

OUTSIDE A ROMAN FORT

Although forts could be as large as 50-60 acres, they were strictly for soldiers and military business. Often, only the bathhouse and an amphitheater were built beyond the walls. The amphitheater was probably used for gladiator fights, parades and ceremonies, of which there were many in the army calendar. After a religious sacrifice the soldiers could feast on the carcasses of the slaughtered animals. Although their diet was good by modern standards – plenty of cereals, fresh fruit and vegetables (when available), and meat from the legion's own herds – it was also boring.

The area surrounding a fort was known as the *canabae* or booths. A large garrison acted as a magnet to local traders and they were allowed to set up their stalls outside a fort. At the stalls and taverns of the *canabae* soldiers enjoyed their leave. When they retired, soldiers were often reluctant to leave the areas they had settled in. They would join their families in their homes near the *canabae*.

Roman soldiers could buy trinkets and treats outside the fort, or get professional letter-writers to send a message home. The booths were strictly controlled by the commander, who had to make sure that the businesses didn't get in the way of the fort's defenses. Eventually, the people from the booths could apply for a charter and become a recognized settlement, or *vicus*. Many towns began like this.

AMPHITHEATER

Bear-baiting, cock-fighting, acrobatics and races were typical events in a regional amphitheater. The chance to see a real gladiator fight was a special occasion. The winning gladiator would ask the crowd if it wanted the loser's life to be spared. The crowd showed their hands and palms up for "yes" and thumbs down for "no."

ROADS AND ENGINEERS

Wherever the Romans went their superb roads followed, and it was soldiers, or slaves supervised by soldiers, who built these arteries of the empire. Always as straight as possible, Roman roads cut through hills and rocks with the aid of tunnels, and crossed rivers with bridges and viaducts. Some were cut into the side of cliffs. Sometimes they were paved with flat stone blocks, at other times with hard-packed gravel. On marshy ground foundations of logs were laid side-by-side under the final surface.

Soldiers at work building a road and in the background an aqueduct. Many of the roads are still in use. It was not until the 18th century that roads of this quality were seen again in Europe. Straight and durable, Roman roads are the most universal and unmistakable evidence of Roman civilization.

BRIDGES

This bridge at Cordoba in Spain is still in use. These military bridges were designed to last. The keystone in the middle of the arch had to be very strong. With so much emphasis on cleanliness and health, the Romans built many aqueducts; artificial channels made of brick, stone or earth for conveying water from rivers to houses and baths.

18

Good roads were essential for the rapid movement of troops and supplies, for trade and for the postal service. Roman roads had frequent milestones and at 12 mile (19km) intervals there were post-houses where travelers could stay overnight and where cavalrymen, the highway patrol, dispatch riders and official travelers could change their horses. On first-class roads there were large hostelries, each a day's journey apart.

At the foot of the Forum in Rome, Augustus had a golden milestone set up. All roads ran toward the heart of the Empire and the Appian Way, which led south of Rome, was the most famous road.

19

RELIGION

The old state religion of the Roman Republic, with Jupiter, Minerva, Vesta and Mars among its chief gods and goddesses, continued under the empire. Instead of regular Sunday services, these deities were sacrificed to on particular occasions. Before a campaign, for example, a public sacrifice might be made to Mars, the god of war. The first emperor, Augustus, was made into a god after he died. In remote parts of the empire officially deified emperors were also worshipped as gods. Within the empire a whole range of religions were allowed as long as they did not openly challenge the official cults and the emperor's divinity. Mithras, a Persian god of light, appealed to soldiers, while the cult of Isis was popular among women in Rome.

Christianity became the official religion of the Roman Empire in the 4th century, during the reign of the Emperor Constantine. He rebuilt Byzantium (Istanbul) and renamed it Constantinople. It eventually became a purely Christian capital for the eastern half of the empire.

Many legionaries followed the cult of Mithras because his cult put great emphasis on comradeship between men. Followers of Mithras were expected to show brotherly love regardless of their status in the world. They met for their ceremonies in caves or in churchlike buildings.

PRIESTS

A priest making a sacrifice. The priests (*haruspices*) attached to each legion supervised the many ceremonies in the official military calendar. The emperor's birthday, or the anniversary of a legion's foundation, for example, would be celebrated by a sacrifice: a bull to Jupiter, a cow to Minerva, a young bull for the emperor.

GOVERNMENT

The Roman Empire had a very flexible system of government. It was divided into provinces under Senate control and provinces that fell under the direct control of the emperor. The older, settled provinces, most of which bordered the Mediterranean, were ruled by proconsuls elected by the Senate, while more newly conquered provinces, such as Britannia, were ruled through legates ("deputies") appointed by the emperor. However, the emperor controlled the senators, a gathering of rich noblemen who filled most of the top posts in government and the army.

Native Romans and Italians took most of the senior administrative jobs until well into the 2nd century. By then, many provincial citizens were working their way up through the rungs of power and by AD 200 just over half of the senators who met in Rome were originally from provinces of the empire. The later emperors Trajan, Hadrian, Antoninus and Marcus Aurelius were descendants of families in Spain and the south of France.

The Emperor Hadrian inspecting one of his outlying forts. Hadrian is famous for having built Hadrian's Wall in England to protect it from northern invasions. He also went on a lengthy tour of the empire to inspect the frontier defenses.

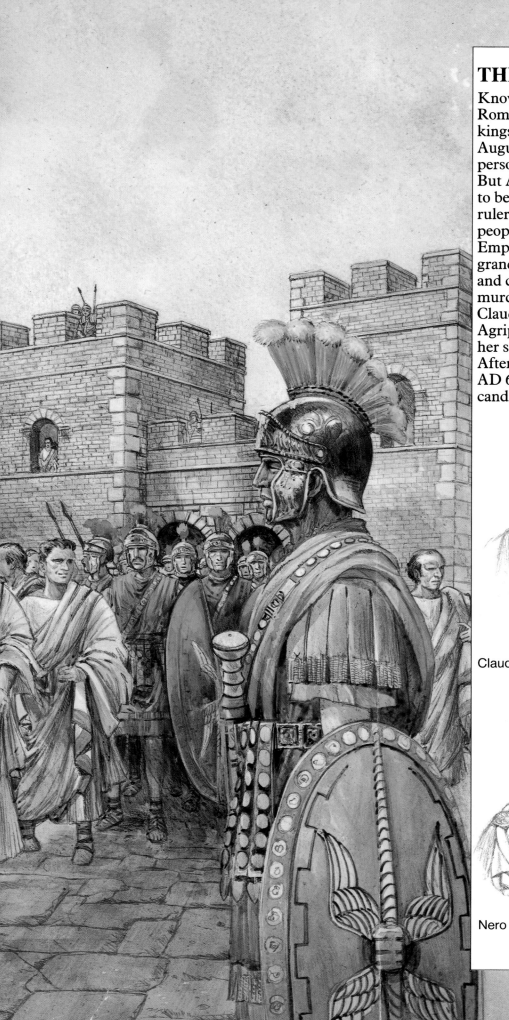

THE EMPERORS

Knowing that the citizens of Rome were suspicious of kings, the first emperor, Augustus, was careful to avoid personal wealth and pomp. But Augustus' successors came to be regarded as supreme rulers, somewhere between the people and the gods. The Emperor Claudius was a grandson of Augustus' wife and came to power after the murder of Caligula by soldiers. Claudius' fourth wife, Agrippina, poisoned him so her son, Nero, would succeed. After Nero killed himself in AD 68 there were four rival candidates.

Augustus

Claudius

Nero

CITIZENS AND SLAVES

During the reign of Augustus, Roman citizenship was a privilege. A citizen of the empire had many legal rights and privileges. Provincials or non-citizens fell under a second-class law called the *ius gentium*. However, early in the 3rd century (AD 211), all free men living within the empire became citizens. By then the empire faced threats from barbarians outside its frontiers and, by giving all men within its frontiers equal rights, hoped to inspire their loyalty.

The Roman Empire depended on millions of slaves, who both in cities and on the land did the hardest and dirtiest work. But even among slaves there were distinctions. Educated Greek slaves were often employed as teachers in noble families. Slaves did much of the clerical and administrative work of the empire. Although they were technically at the mercy of their owners, by imperial times slaves had some rights against unjust or brutal masters. More important, they could expect to become freedmen eventually.

Rome offered an orderly, prosperous life as a citizen while invading barbarians offered chaos. If a treaty could not be made, or if they could not be encouraged to settle peacefully in a fixed place within the empire, these war-like land-hungry tribes had to be overcome militarily.

THE *TOGA*

The *toga*, a half circle of white wool or linen wrapped around the body with the end carried over the left arm, was the badge of Roman citizenship. It was hard to wear properly without pins or buttons, and it was so cumbersome and difficult to keep clean that in the days of the empire it was only worn on public and formal occasions. A great event in the life of a Roman boy was the day on which, about his 15th year, he put on the *toga virilis*, the toga of manhood. He went to the Forum where he was congratulated and his name was then added to the list of citizens.

WHAT BECAME OF ROMAN FORTS?

Under Trajan (AD 98-117) the empire grew too big to be easily defended. The next emperor, Hadrian, gave up some of Trajan's conquests and concentrated on strengthening existing boundaries.

At this time the empire was at its most peaceful and stable, but this situation did not continue. The third century saw frequent strife and disaster. The most heavily manned forts could not keep out invasions by masses of people forever. Germanic tribes were pushing over the Rhine, while Persians were pushing in from the east.

In AD 285 the emperor Diocletian had to introduce a totally new system of government. The empire was divided into eastern and western parts. Emperors had to be full-time military leaders and the army became weakened by the constant wars. In 410 the Visigoths invaded Italy and sacked Rome. Then in 476 the last western emperor, Romulus Augustulus, was deposed by his German commanders. Only the eastern half of the empire, with its capital of Constantinople, endured until its capture by Turks, in 1453.

The Romans occasionally used existing hill-forts as the basis for their own forts. When the Roman soldiers dismantled or abandoned their forts, the local people would then take over the sites and build their own towns round them.

HADRIAN'S WALL

Hadrian's Wall, which runs for 70 miles from Wallsend-on-Tyne to Bowness-on-Solway, was built in the AD 120s after a visit by the Emperor. He streamlined the empire and was concerned to protect this most northerly defense from attack by Picts. The wall was 9 feet thick and 19 feet high. It had 80 small castles and a fort every 4-6 miles. It was overrun several times, and had to be rebuilt before being abandoned in the 4th century.

THE ROMAN EMPIRE TODAY

When the empire had split in two, and its western half had collapsed, so did the legal system and the far-reaching trading networks. Rome was no longer the imperial capital and imperial buildings fell into ruins.

But, in addition to the enduring Roman legacy of Christianity, the empire lived on in countless other ways. Many modern languages – Italian, French, Spanish, Romanian – grew from a common Latin source. Latin words make up more than half of the words we use in English and came via the Normans. Among them are the words and phrases that are just the same today as they were two thousand years ago: when we speak of the salary a person receives *per annum*, for example. Then there are words that we use without realizing their origins. Arena, for example, means "sand" since the amphitheaters were usually covered with sand. Other ordinary everyday examples are "omen," "specimen," "actor," and "circus." In Britain place-names ending in "chester" come from *castrum* (camp).

For centuries and centuries after the death of the last western emperor, Rome continued to be a civilizing influence. Ruins like Dougga in Tunisia remained as a physical reminder of its grandeur, while the cultural and political legacy has been permanent.

ROMAN INFLUENCE

When people think of civilization, classical Roman buildings come to mind. Architects have continued to draw inspiration from Roman buildings. Churches were built with Roman arches throughout Europe until a new Gothic style of pointed arches became widely used in the 11th century. This library building at Oxford in England clearly owes a lot to Roman design. The founders of modern America were also influenced by Roman civilization. They used words like "senate," "constitution" and "republic."

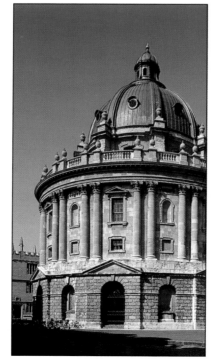

DATE CHARTS

31 BC Victory for Octavian at the Battle of Actium

27 Octavian becomes Augustus and the Roman empire begins

6 AD Judea made a Roman province

14 Death of Augustus

c. 28 Crucifixion of Jesus Christ

41 Emperor Caligula murdered by Praetorians

43 Roman conquest of southern Britain

64 Great fire of Rome

66 Jews in Palestine revolt against Roman rule

68 Death of Nero

70 Jewish revolt suppressed

79 Destruction of Pompeii by eruption of Vesuvius

80 Completion of the Colosseum in Rome

117 Death of Trajan; accession of Hadrian. Roman empire at its greatest extent

122 Beginning of Hadrian's Wall

161-66 War against the Parthians, followed by plague

212 Edict of Caracalla grants Roman citizenship on all free male inhabitants of the empire

230s onwards Wars with Persia. Barbarian invasions across Rhine and Danube

253-68 Germanic barbarians invade the empire

284 Accession of

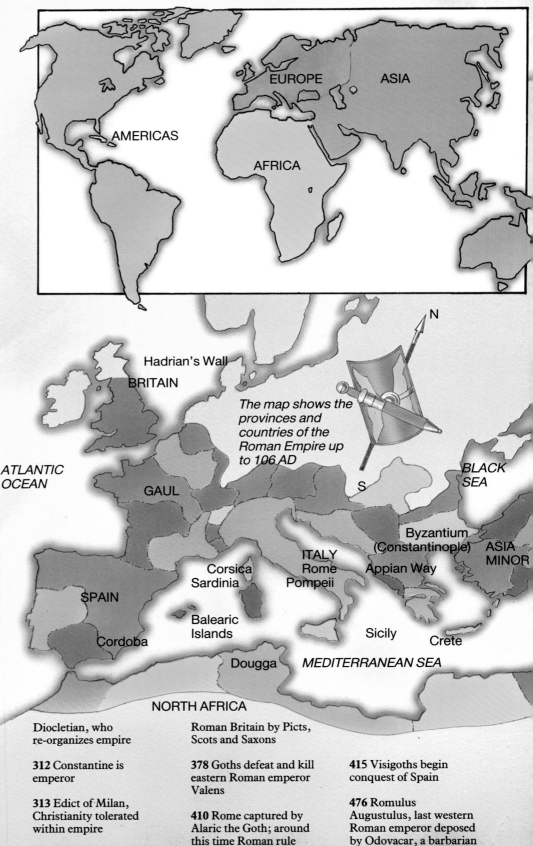

The map shows the provinces and countries of the Roman Empire up to 106 AD

EUROPE

ASIA

AMERICAS

AFRICA

N

Hadrian's Wall

BRITAIN

ATLANTIC OCEAN

GAUL

S

BLACK SEA

SPAIN

Corsica
Sardinia

ITALY
Rome
Pompeii

Byzantium (Constantinople)

Appian Way

ASIA MINOR

Cordoba

Balearic Islands

Sicily

Crete

Dougga

MEDITERRANEAN SEA

NORTH AFRICA

Diocletian, who re-organizes empire

312 Constantine is emperor

313 Edict of Milan, Christianity tolerated within empire

367 Successful attack on

Roman Britain by Picts, Scots and Saxons

378 Goths defeat and kill eastern Roman emperor Valens

410 Rome captured by Alaric the Goth; around this time Roman rule ends in Britain

415 Visigoths begin conquest of Spain

476 Romulus Augustulus, last western Roman emperor deposed by Odovacar, a barbarian leader

30

AFRICA	ASIA	AMERICAS	EUROPE
		100 BC Beginning of the rise of Teotihuacan, great city in Mexico	
			27 BC Octavian becomes emperor; the Roman empire begins
6 AD Judea made a Roman province	6 AD Civil service examination system begins in China		
	8 Radical reforms by Emperor Wang Mang in China		
10 Kushite kingdom in Nubea in decline	25 Beginning of Han dynasty in China		14 AD Augustus dies
c33 Crucifixion of Jesus Christ	c58-75 Buddhism accepted as official religion in China		64 Great fire of Rome
66 Jews in Palestine revolt against Roman rule			79 Destruction of Pompeii by eruption of Vesuvius
70 Jewish revolt suppressed	97 Chinese expedition under Kang Hin to Persian Cult		
	c100 Mongol invaders bring rice and iron to Japan; paper invented in China		117 Death of Trajan; accession of Hadrian
			161-66 The Romans fight the Parthians
			212 Edict of Caracalla gives Roman citizenship to all free men in the empire
	220 End of Han dynasty in China		230s onward Wars with Persia; barbarian invasions across the Danube and Rhine
	230 Emperor Sujin rules Japan; first written records there		253-68 Germanic barbarians invade the empire
c300 Axum conquers Nubia and becomes the dominant power in the Red Sea	309-79 Persian power at its height under Shapur II	300 AD Classic Mayan civilization established in Mesoamerica	284 Diocletian begins to re-organize the empire
	320 Gupta dynasty reunites India		313 Edict of Milan, Christianity tolerated within empire
	c350 Pallava dynasty set up in south India		
400 Axum converts to Christianity	c360 Japan conquers Korea	c400 Incas start to establish themselves on the South American coast	410 Rome captured by Alaric the Goth
429 Vandal kingdom of North Africa is set up			476 Romulus Augustulus, last Western Roman emperor deposed by Odovacar
560 Birth of Muhammad			

GLOSSARY

canabae "booths," the settlement around a fort

castrum "camp"

century a unit of the Roman army consisting of 80 men

cohort six centuries or 480 men. A legion had ten cohorts

haruspices the priests attached to legions

ius gentium the legal system of non-citizens

papilio "butterfly," the nickname for an army tent

Pax Romana "Roman Peace"

praetorium the commander's house in a fort

principia headquarters in a camp or fort

sacellum the shrine in which legionary standards were kept

tessera waxed wooden tablet on which the daily password was written; the *tesserius* was the officer in charge of the passwords.

toga virilis "toga of manhood" worn by Roman boys at their coming of age

vicus a permanent settlement of retired soldiers

INDEX

Photographic credits:
Pages 9, 12, 16, 18, 25 and 28: Michael Holford Photography; page 20: Werner Forman Archive; pages 27 and the back cover: J. Allan Cash Library.

CHILDREN'S ROOM

DATE DUE

DEMCO